Messages of

Letting Go

for **Lent 2021**

D0775621

Messages of

Letting Go

for **Lent 2021**

3-MINUTE DEVOTIONS

MICHAEL WHITE and **TOM CORCORAN**

AVE MARIA PRESS · AVE · Notre Dame, Indiana

Responsorial psalms are excerpted from the *Lectionary for Mass for Use in the Dioceses of the United States of America, second typical edition* © 2001, 1998, 1997, 1986, 1970 Confraternity of Christian Doctrine, Inc., Washington, DC. Used with permission. All rights reserved. No portion of this text may be reproduced by any means without permission in writing from the copyright owner.

Scripture texts in this work are taken from the *New American Bible, revised edition* © 2010, 1991, 1986, 1970 Confraternity of Christian Doctrine, Washington, DC, and are used by permission of the copyright owner. All Rights Reserved. No part of the *New American Bible* may be reproduced in any form without permission in writing from the copyright owner.

© 2020 by Michael White and Tom Corcoran

All rights reserved. No part of this book may be used or reproduced in any manner whatsoever, except in the case of reprints in the context of reviews, without written permission from Ave Maria Press®, Inc., P.O. Box 428, Notre Dame, IN 46556, 1-800-282-1865.

Founded in 1865, Ave Maria Press is a ministry of the United States Province of Holy Cross.

www.avemariapress.com

Paperback: ISBN-13 978-1-64680-005-6

E-book: ISBN-13 978-1-64680-006-3

Cover and text design by Samantha Watson.

Printed and bound in the United States of America.

Introduction

The dictionary defines an offense as "a breach of a law or rule; an illegal act." It also defines an offense as "an annoyance or resentment brought about by a perceived insult to or disregard for oneself."

Offenses are inevitable.

There are two kinds of offenses: perceived and real. Some offenses that we experience offend us based on our sensibilities, our past wounds, or our opinions. They offend us for sure, but no real harm or injury was intended. We may feel offended because someone challenges our own self-image or perceived identity. The other person hit a nerve. For example, if you are a parent you may get very easily offended if a teacher, relative, or friend says anything critical about your child. Whether they are right or have a legitimate insight is irrelevant. Offense can be taken concerning our clothes or appearance, our height or weight, our position or accomplishments. The list goes on and on. Most of the time these offenses are unintended, but it would be naïve not to acknowledge other times when the offense is quite deliberate, intended to inflict pain. Either way, offenses are inevitable, and they hurt.

Every offense we experience is an opportunity for us to step back and evaluate the offense. This is important because of the second major fact about offenses: offenses are a trap.

Every offense is a trap that can impede us and keep us from living up to our full potential. Did you ever notice that an offended person lives with a huge sense of entitlement? Everyone owes him or her something. They are owed an apology or some other kind of recompense, and they seem to be waiting around for it. As a result, they get stuck. They spend too much time playing the victim and waiting for others to fix the offense rather than actually living their lives.

We can fall into that trap too. Living in offense is a trap that will rob us of what God wants for us. The fruit of offense is hurt, outrage, jealousy, resentment, strife, bitterness, hatred, and envy. When we take offense and then hold it in our hearts, we allow these toxins to grow within us. If we make it a habit to internalize offenses and not deal with them in a healthy way, we will become angry people.

God has a different vision for us. God wants us to live a life of love, joy, peace, patience, kindness, goodness, gentleness, faithfulness, and self-control. These are the fruits of living connected to God's Holy Spirit (see Gal 5:22–23), and they are the opposite of living offended.

This leads to a third fact about offenses: We can choose how we handle them. When we *feel* offended or *are* offended, we can choose to repent or turn away from the offense and turn back to God. We can choose healthy responses that draw us closer to God, strengthen our character, and make us more loving people.

Every Lenten season calls us to repent. We are to turn away from sin and selfishness and turn back to our loving God. We can choose to repent of the times in the past and in the present that we have chosen to hold onto an offense rather than let it go.

We pray that this book will help you take that journey of repentance this Lenten season so you can cast off offense and live in the truth of God's love and goodness.

Fr. Michael and Tom

WEEK OF
Ash Wednesday

Wednesday, February 17

Yet even now—oracle of the LORD—
    return to me with your whole heart,
    with fasting, weeping, and mourning.
Rend your hearts, not your garments,
    and return to the LORD, your God,
For he is gracious and merciful,
    slow to anger, abounding in steadfast love,
    and relenting in punishment.
Perhaps he will again relent
    and leave behind a blessing,

—Joel 2:12–14a

The prophet Joel speaks for the Lord and asks the people of Israel to return to the Lord. In their return, the Lord calls the people to rend their hearts and not their garments. The tearing of garments was a sign of repentance. Instead of just an outward sign of repentance, the Lord desires a change of heart.

As we begin our Lenten journey, we can be focused on outside appearances. We can be caught up in the externals and lose the purpose of our fasting and giving and sacrifices. The point is a change of heart. We want to rend or rip out of our hearts the envy, anger, or bitterness that has settled into them so that God can fill us with his grace and mercy and kindness. As we remove offenses from our hearts we will experience blessing from the Lord.

....

Ask God to help you return to him with your whole heart this Lent and to remove any offenses you have carried in your heart.

Thursday, February 18

So we are ambassadors for Christ, as if God were appealing through us. We implore you on behalf of Christ, be reconciled to God. For our sake he made him to be sin who did not know sin, so that we might become the righteousness of God in him.
—2 Corinthians 5:20–21

Jesus came to earth and went to the Cross so that we would be reconciled to God. Jesus went to the Cross and suffered the consequences of sin so that we might be made righteous with God. His work on the Cross puts us in right relationship with our heavenly Father. His work allows us to get rid of all the sin and ugliness in our hearts.

When we get offended, we sometimes choose to hold onto anger, bitterness, and pride. None of this puts us in right relationship with God, others, or ourselves. It only serves to alienate us from others.

....

Take a moment to acknowledge a desire for reconciliation with God the Father through Jesus Christ. Thank him that he sent his Son to die for you. Pray for the grace to get rid of the toxins of offense.

Friday, February 19

[Jesus said to his disciples,] "Take care not to perform righteous deeds in order that people may see them; otherwise, you will have no recompense from your heavenly Father. When you give alms, do not blow a trumpet before you, as the hypocrites do in the synagogues and in the streets to win the praise of others. Amen, I say to you, they have received their reward. But when you give alms, do not let your left hand know what your right is doing, so that your almsgiving may be secret. And your Father who sees in secret will repay you."

—Matthew 6:1–4

Jesus teaches his followers not to practice righteous deeds publicly for the purpose of human accolades and attention. For example, they are not to let everyone know when they give money to the poor. When they do that they will be rewarded, but the reward will only come from human beings. On the other hand, when we give quietly and secretly, we will receive a reward from our heavenly Father.

The rewards from our heavenly Father are rewards of the heart. Jesus tells us to do good deeds quietly because it is in secret that our heavenly Father can give us the gifts of joy, peace, and his grace in our hearts. Jesus always looks at our hearts and is after the renovation of our hearts.

Ask Jesus to come into your heart right now. Pray that you will do your Lenten practices for the purpose of internal change and the good of others, not for worldly accolades.

Saturday, February 20

Psalm 86:1–2, 3–4, 5–6

Teach me your way, O Lord, that I may walk in your truth.

Incline your ear, O LORD; answer me,
    for I am afflicted and poor.
Keep my life, for I am devoted to you;
    save your servant who trusts in you.
    You are my God.

Teach me your way, O Lord, that I may walk in your truth.

Have mercy on me, O Lord,
    for to you I call all the day.
Gladden the soul of your servant,
    for to you, O Lord, I lift up my soul.

Teach me your way, O Lord, that I may walk in your truth.

For you, O LORD, are good and forgiving,
    abounding in kindness to all who call upon
        you.
Hearken, O LORD, to my prayer
    and attend to the sound of my pleading.

Teach me your way, O Lord, that I may walk in your truth.

First Week

OF LENT

Sunday, February 21

The first Sunday of Lent always focuses on Jesus' temptation in the desert. Temptations are a part of life, no matter how mature we are in our faith. No matter how spiritually mature you are you will be tempted. Temptation is not a sign of spiritual immaturity. It is a sign that you are human. The difference between spiritually immature people and spiritually mature people is that spiritually mature people know how they are tempted. They know the environments or situations or issues that tempt them and can lead them into sin.

When it comes to getting offended, we all have different ways in which we are tempted. What easily offends you will not easily offend me. A sensitive topic for me may not mean anything to you. To grow spiritually, we must become more aware of ourselves and what will lead us into feeling offended.

....

Pray today for the grace to know yourself better. Ask the Holy Spirit to reveal to you the issues that tempt you into offense. Ask the Holy Spirit to give you knowledge, understanding, and wisdom about those issues.

Monday, February 22

At once the Spirit drove him out into the desert, and he remained in the desert for forty days, tempted by Satan.

—Mark 1:12–13a

Jesus was tempted even though he was following the direction of the Holy Spirit. He didn't get tempted because he was apart from God's will, but because he was in it. We should avoid situations that lead us into unnecessary temptation, but we will never be able to avoid temptation completely.

Inevitably, we will be offended by others and tempted to harbor the offense, internalize it, and allow it to live in our hearts. If we allow it in, we risk becoming entitled, bitter, and self-centered people. The fruit of living with an offended heart is never good.

....

Pray today for the grace to recognize the temptation to harbor and nurture offense. Pray for a humble heart that is not so sensitive and easily offended.

Tuesday, February 23

This is the time of fulfillment. The kingdom of God is at hand. Repent, and believe in the gospel.
—Mark 1:15

After Jesus is tempted in the desert, he announces his basic message: The kingdom of God is at hand. God's kingdom is not some faraway place but something we can experience in the here and now. God's kingdom is the place where God rules people's hearts and lives. To enter the kingdom, we simply need to repent and believe the Good News.

To repent means to turn away from whatever bad and unhealthy habits we have formed and turn back to God. To repent means to turn away from self-defeating behaviors and turn back to God's goodness and grace. We can repent of focusing on the offenses we have received and instead put our focus on the Good News of God's love for us.

....

Take a moment to repent of any times you have harbored and held on to an offense. Tell God that you do not want it in your heart and confess your belief in the Good News of God's love.

Wednesday, February 24

This is the time of fulfillment. The kingdom of God is at hand. Repent, and believe in the good news.
—Mark 1:15

Even if we allow offense into our hearts, we can choose to repent and believe in the Good News:

Repent of harboring offense and believe the Good News that Christ died for you.

Repent and believe the Good News that God is for you even when others are against you.

Repent and believe the Good News that even though others don't always treat you as you deserve, God has treated you better than you deserve—not counting your offenses against you but treating you with mercy and kindness.

Repent of your unrealistic expectations for others and believe the Good News that God can give us infinitely more than we can ask or imagine.

Repent of your need for life to always be easy and getting offended when it's not and believe the Good News that God makes all things work together for your good.

Repent of the offense you take when the world doesn't revolve around you and believe the Good News that you get to live for God's eternal purposes.

....

Take a look at the list above. Confess to God the ways you need to repent of any offense and replace it with the Good News of the Gospel.

Thursday, February 25

Be angry but do not sin; do not let the sun set on
your anger, and do not leave room for the devil.
—Ephesians 4:26–27

Paul writes to the Ephesians to teach them about
how to live in community with one another. He
tells them that it is OK to be angry, but it is not
OK to sin. They can get angry and still choose to
avoid sin. He then says they should get rid of their
anger quickly because anger gives the devil room
to work in their lives.

When we get offended, it often turns to anger.
If we do not deal with the anger of being offended, we give the devil and evil spirits room in our
hearts to make us bitter, entitled, and self-centered.
It is how marriages are destroyed and relationships
are ended.

....

Have you let the sun set on a past offense? Has it
brought about bitterness? If so, repent of it. Ask God
for his mercy and grace to bring healing to your heart.

Friday, February 26

All bitterness, fury, anger, shouting, and reviling must be removed from you, along with all malice. [And] be kind to one another, compassionate, forgiving one another as God has forgiven you in Christ.

—Ephesians 4:31–32

Paul continues to give wisdom to the Ephesians about how to build a healthy Christian community. He tells them to get rid of all bitterness, fury, anger, and shouting at one another. These are the natural reactions that come from being offended, but we shouldn't let them take root in our hearts. Instead, Paul offers an alternative to these reactions: he says to replace those actions with kindness and compassion and with forgiving one another as God has forgiven us. These are not our natural reactions to offenses, and nurturing them takes work, but they are a healthier response to offenses for both ourselves and others than our natural responses are.

....

When we are offended, we can choose to be kind, compassionate, and forgiving, and we can choose not to nurture the offense. Pray today for the grace to extend kindness, compassion, and forgiveness—rather than anger or shouting—toward the people who offend you.

Saturday, February 27

Psalm 119:1–2, 4–5, 7–8

Blessed are they who follow the law of the Lord!

Blessed are they whose way is blameless,
  who walk in the law of the LORD.
Blessed are they who observe his decrees,
  who seek him with all their heart.

Blessed are they who follow the law of the Lord!

You have commanded that your precepts
  be diligently kept.
Oh, that I might be firm in the ways
  of keeping your statutes!

Blessed are they who follow the law of the Lord!

I will give you thanks with an upright heart,
  when I have learned your just ordinances.
I will keep your statutes;
  do not utterly forsake me.

Blessed are they who follow the law of the Lord!

Second Week

OF LENT

Sunday, February 28

While offenses are inevitable, we can choose how to handle them. Rather than nurturing an offense, we can handle it in a healthy way.

One healthy way to handle offenses is to put them in the proper perspective. When we experience an offense, it feels all-encompassing, as if it is our only reality or the most real thing in the world. In this week of Lent we will consider words from St. Paul that help us put offenses in the proper perspective.

....

Pray today for the grace to see the offenses you suffer from the proper perspective.

Monday, March 1

We know that all things work for good for those who love God, who are called according to his purpose.
—Romans 8:28

Paul says that in everything that happens to us, God works for good for those who love him. Do you know what "everything" means in the original Greek? It means *everything*. In everything that happens to us, God is working for good.

Paul does not say that everything that happens in life is good. Clearly, that is not true. There is evil in the world. But Paul is saying that in every situation, God is working on our behalf to bring about something good. Anyone can bring good out of good. God brings good out of evil, but we have to cooperate with him. We have to work *with* him. We have to be on the lookout for how to work with God so that he can bring good out of the offenses we suffer.

....

Pray today for the perspective that God can bring good out of any offenses that you suffer.

Tuesday, March 2

We know that all things work for good for those who love God, who are called according to his purpose. For those he foreknew he also predestined to be conformed to the image of his Son, so that he might be the firstborn among many brothers.

—Romans 8:28–29

God brings good out of bad situations in our lives. Sometimes we don't get what we want; our plans don't work out, and then we realize that God protected us from a bad relationship, a bad business partnership, a bad deal or situation. God protected us from being in the wrong place at the wrong time. Sometimes God makes our situation better, but in every situation, good and bad, God is working to bring about goodness in our character. He is working to change us from the inside out.

In all situations, he is working to make us more like his Son. Our circumstances are not any better, but God is using a situation to grow our character so that we will conform to the image and character of Jesus. That's what Paul is talking about here.

When it comes to offenses, God wants to use them so that we become more like Jesus. He is using them to help us grow in patience, kindness, goodness, and understanding of others.

Pray today that you would use offenses to grow to be more like Jesus.

Wednesday, March 3

We know that all things work for good for those who love God, who are called according to his purpose. For those he foreknew he also predestined to be conformed to the image of his Son, so that he might be the firstborn among many brothers. . . .
What then shall we say to this? If God is for us, who can be against us?

—Romans 8:28–29, 31

Paul writes that God can make all things work together for our good. God brings good out of evil, and in every situation, if we are working with him, we can grow to have a character like Jesus. Then he asks a rhetorical question: If God is for us, who can be against us?

If God is for us then people being against us or acting against us is nothing in comparison. When others offend us or are insensitive to us, their actions pale in comparison to God's goodness and God's ability to bring good out of a bad situation. God's grace and power are greater than any offense others can level at you. Even if someone gossips about you, speaks poorly about you, criticizes you, or insults you, God is for you. God is working for your good. And nothing, absolutely nothing, they do can keep God from bringing good out of the situation, except you.

Pray today for the grace to know that in every situation, God is for you. Confess your belief in that truth to God today.

Thursday, March 4

What then shall we say to this? If God is for us, who can be against us? He who did not spare his own Son but handed him over for us all, will he not also give us everything else along with him?

—Romans 8:31–32

God held nothing back when he sent Jesus to die for our sins. He gave us his very best. He gave up what he loved most to wipe away our sins and our offenses so that we could have a relationship with him. And so God isn't going to hold out on us or fail to give us what we need.

We can rest secure in that truth.

Whenever we get sucked into allowing an offense to define us or to command all of our attention, we need to pull back and say, "Wait a minute. Time out." The offense does not have the final word. The offense doesn't define us. The offense doesn't have to control our lives. Even though another person has overlooked us or slighted us or treated us poorly, God does not overlook us. God will not slight us. God always treats us with dignity and respect and is always working for our good.

....

Pray today that when the lie of offense makes you think that the offense is your greatest reality, you will remember that you belong to God and that he is always working for your good.

Friday, March 5

> But Joseph replied to them: "Do not fear. Can I take the place of God? Even though you meant to harm me, God meant it for good, to achieve this present end, the survival of many people."
>
> —Genesis 50:19–20

God makes all things work together for our good. Perhaps no story from scripture better displays this truth than the story of Joseph. Joseph was betrayed by his brothers and sold into slavery. Rather than nurture the offense, he did his best in every situation. Eventually, Joseph rose to be the second in command of Egypt. He successfully managed the resources of the land during a time of plenty in preparation for a time of famine.

Eventually Joseph's brothers came to him for food, although they didn't recognize him until Joseph revealed himself. Rather than exacting revenge on his brothers, Joseph recognized that God brought good out of the situation to save many people. What his brothers intended for evil, God used for good.

....

God can use whatever offense you are nurturing and holding in your heart to bring about a great good. Pray today for the perspective of Joseph.

Saturday, March 6

Psalm 116:10, 15, 16–17, 18–19
I will walk before the Lord, in the land of the living.
I believed, even when I said,
 "I am greatly afflicted."
Precious in the eyes of the LORD
 is the death of his faithful ones.
I will walk before the Lord, in the land of the living.
O LORD, I am your servant;
 I am your servant, the son of your handmaid;
 you have loosed my bonds.
To you will I offer sacrifice of thanksgiving,
and I will call upon the name of the LORD.
I will walk before the Lord, in the land of the living.
My vows to the LORD I will pay
 in the presence of all his people,
In the courts of the house of the LORD,
 in your midst, O Jerusalem.
I will walk before the Lord, in the land of the living.

Third Week

OF LENT

Sunday, March 7

Offenses are sometimes the result of things we don't want to but need to hear. In these instances, instead of nurturing the offense, we can choose to respond in a healthy way.

In this third week of Lent, we are looking at the times we are offended by the truth. To be successful in life, we must learn to receive the truth without being offended by it. Facts are our friends. The truth is our ally. If people do not give us truthful feedback because they fear offending us, we will greatly limit our opportunities for personal development and growth.

....

Pray today to overcome any offense you take at hearing feedback or being confronted with the truth.

Monday, March 8

Since the Passover of the Jews was near, Jesus went up to Jerusalem. He found in the temple area those who sold oxen, sheep, and doves, as well as the money-changers seated there.

—John 2:13–14

Pious and practicing Jewish people of Jesus' time would go to Jerusalem during Passover to celebrate the feast. The population in Jerusalem would swell by tens of thousands of people as pilgrims from all over the surrounding area would come to the Temple to worship God and offer sacrifices. Jesus was one of those people.

When Jesus arrived, he saw in the outer courts animals being sold and money-changers exchanging Temple coins for Roman coinage. This part of the Temple was known as the Porch of Solomon, the eastern side of the Court of the Gentiles. It was the only place the Gentiles or non-Jewish people were allowed to go to pray. But they couldn't pray because of all the buying and selling of goods. The merchants quite simply didn't belong there.

....

What is in your life right now that doesn't belong? Pray for the grace to spot it or for the humility to listen to others when they challenge you to drive bad things out of your life.

Tuesday, March 9

He made a whip out of cords and drove them all out of the temple area, with the sheep and the oxen, and spilled the coins of the money-changers and overturned their tables, and to those who sold doves, he said, "Take these out of here, and stop making my Father's house a marketplace."
—John 2:15–16

Jesus comes to the Temple and sees merchants selling sheep and oxen for sacrifice at exorbitant prices, taking advantage of people. He also sees that they are buying and selling in the outer courtyard, interfering with Gentiles who are praying.

Jesus turns over the tables and yells at the merchants and money-changers to get out of his Father's house because they are making it a place of business rather than a place of worship. They are using God to make a profit while getting in the way of people worshipping. He offers some very strong and unequivocal feedback that this is unacceptable.

....

When there is evil in our lives or something we are doing wrong, feedback can feel very unwelcome—as if someone is overturning everything in our lives. Pray for the grace to get over those feelings and lean into honest feedback.

Wednesday, March 10

At this the Jews answered and said to him, "What sign can you show for doing this?" Jesus answered and said to them, "Destroy this temple and in three days I will raise it up."

—John 2:18–19

Now it was an obvious fact that the Jewish leaders had made the Temple into a marketplace. It was right out there in plain sight. However, rather than acknowledging the truth of the situation, the religious leaders get offended by Jesus' actions. They demand a sign from him.

This is in an interesting response because the prophet Malachi had predicted that the Messiah would come into the Temple one day and cleanse it of corruption. So they knew what they were doing was not right, but instead of admitting it, they challenged Jesus and his authority.

When we are offended by the truth, we often deflect constructive criticism. We will point fingers or make excuses or challenge the person pointing out the truth, as the religious leaders did. These tactics may distract others, but they do nothing to help us grow into the people God created us to be.

....

Pray today for the grace to receive helpful feedback rather than deflect it.

Thursday, March 11

Hence, now there is no condemnation for those who are in Christ Jesus.

—Romans 8:1

Honest feedback is a gift that helps you to grow. It is your number one tool for personal and professional growth. Feedback is the breakfast of champions and successful people. To see feedback as a present, separate it from your identity. Separate the "do" from the "who."

One of the reasons we see feedback and facts as enemies is because we think of them as comments on who we are instead of what we do. We are confronted with a brutal fact and feel like it is a commentary on our value as a person.

When you feel condemned by feedback or facts, call to mind the verse above. There is no condemnation for those in Christ Jesus. The facts are not a comment on who you are as a person. No facts can condemn you or change your identity in Christ.

....

Take a moment to memorize Romans 8:1. Pray for the grace to remember this verse when you receive unpleasant feedback.

Friday, March 12

The way of fools is right in their own eyes,
but those who listen to advice are the wise.
—Proverbs 12:15

Proverbs tells us that fools are right in their own eyes. In other words, they think because they do something it must be right. Fools never take time to consider life from a perspective other than their own. As a result, they don't grow.

On the other hand, wise people listen to advice. Proverbs does not say wise people take advice but that they listen to it and they grow. In the same way, we can listen to criticism and feedback, and even if we determine it isn't true or doesn't apply to us, we grow and learn from the simple process of listening.

....

Pray today for the grace to listen to advice and input from others and not get offended.

Saturday, March 13

Psalm 51:3–4, 18–19, 20–21ab
It is mercy I desire, and not sacrifice.
Have mercy on me, O God, in your goodness;
    in the greatness of your compassion wipe out
        my offense.
Thoroughly wash me from my guilt
    and of my sin cleanse me.
It is mercy I desire, and not sacrifice.
For you are not pleased with sacrifices;
    should I offer a burnt offering, you would not
        accept it.
My sacrifice, O God, is a contrite spirit;
    a heart contrite and humbled, O God, you will
        not spurn.
It is mercy I desire, and not sacrifice.
Be bountiful, O LORD, to Zion in your kindness
    by rebuilding the walls of Jerusalem;
Then shall you be pleased with due sacrifices,
    burnt offerings and holocausts.
It is mercy I desire, and not sacrifice.

Fourth Week

OF LENT

Sunday, March 14

This week we are looking at real offenses we suffer from others. In this sin-stained world, people will cheat, steal from, and harm us. No one gets out of this world without being harmed and offended by others.

In order to get real offenses out of our hearts, we have to forgive others. We can forgive others' offenses because Jesus forgave ours. Forgiveness is not saying the offense didn't matter; it isn't saying you trust the person who hurt you. Forgiveness simply means to cancel a debt. The person who offends you doesn't owe you any longer.

....

Pray today for the grace to be able to forgive others as Christ has forgiven you.

Monday, March 15

You were dead in your transgressions and sins in which you once lived following the age of this world, following the ruler of the power of the air, the spirit that is now at work in the disobedient.

—Ephesians 2:1–2

Paul writes to the Ephesians helping them understand the reality of their spiritual condition before their relationship with Christ. He tells them that they were dead in their transgressions and following the spirit of disobedience that led away from God.

Like the Ephesians, we have all been dead in our transgressions and sins. Sin doesn't make you bad. It makes you dead. Sin kills your soul. Sin kills relationships with others. Sin kills our relationship with God and disconnects us from him.

God's laws cannot be broken. When we transgress God's laws and commands for how to live we don't break his laws, we break ourselves against the laws. And so we need to be saved from and forgiven for this.

....

Pray today for a clear understanding of how sin kills your relationships with God and others so that you will avoid it in the future.

Tuesday, March 16

All of us once lived among them in the desires of our flesh, following the wishes of the flesh and the impulses, and we were by nature children of wrath, like the rest.

—Ephesians 2:3

Paul continues to describe our spiritual condition apart from Christ. He writes that all of us have lived according to the desires of our flesh. By "flesh," Paul doesn't mean our bodies but our sinful nature or the inclination toward evil living in us. We have all disregarded God's teachings because we wanted to do what felt good to us. We felt the impulses to lie, cheat, steal, gossip, and speak poorly about others and gave into those impulses.

Think of how you would feel if a good friend of yours was in need, and you gave them a lot of money or a job opportunity and then he or she never said thank you. Or, what if they ignored you all the time and didn't answer your texts or phone calls?

This is our reality. When we harm or injure others and ignore God, we offend him. And God would be perfectly justified in responding to us with wrath, with anger. That is what each of us deserves from God.

....

Repent today of any times you have offended God by ignoring him or doing only what you want to do. Thank God that he treats you not based on what you have done but on what his Son has done for you on the Cross.

Wednesday, March 17

All of us once lived among them in the desires of our flesh, following the wishes of the flesh and the impulses, and we were by nature children of wrath, like the rest. But God, who is rich in mercy, because of the great love he had for us, even when we were dead in our transgressions, brought us to life with Christ.

—Ephesians 2:3–5

The whole wave of action and direction of Paul's letter is toward the justifiable wrath of God. We deserve God's wrath. We deserve to pay for our sins and for offending God. That's what we would expect from any human person. However, Paul then changes direction completely with two simple words: *But God.*

While from any human being we would expect to be paid back for our sins or treated as we treated them, God acts completely differently. When we offended God, God didn't pay us back; he brought us back. He brought us back to life through the death and Resurrection of his Son.

....

Thank God today that he doesn't treat you as you deserve but instead has brought you back to life through Christ.

Thursday, March 18

For by grace you have been saved through faith, and this is not from you; it is the gift of God. It is not from works, so no one may boast.

—Ephesians 2:8–9

God forgave us our sins and brought us back to life. Sin had destroyed our souls and ruined our relationship with God. There was nothing we could do on our own to save ourselves, but God decided to bring us back to life. It is a gift. It is all grace.

Paul wants us to be very clear that we have nothing to do with getting into a right relationship with God. It is all God's work. You cannot boast of anything you have done to get into a right relationship with God.

And when it comes to getting into heaven, God doesn't add up all the good things you did and then subtract all the bad you did and if the good outweighs the bad you get in, and if the bad outweighs the good you don't. We can't earn heaven. We can only receive it like a little child.

....

Thank God today for the free gift of salvation in Jesus Christ.

Friday, March 19

All bitterness, fury, anger, shouting, and reviling must be removed from you, along with all malice. [And] be kind to one another, compassionate, forgiving one another as God has forgiven you in Christ.

—Ephesians 4:31–32

God has forgiven us in Jesus Christ. And so if we want to get rid of bitterness, anger, and malice, we have to forgive others as Christ has forgiven us. Who do you need to forgive as Christ has forgiven you?

....

Name the offense and what they took from you. Cancel the debt. Announce that they don't owe you anymore. Ask Jesus to come and heal your heart.

Saturday, March 20

Psalm 7:2–3, 9bc–10, 11–12
O Lord, my God, in you I take refuge.
O Lord, my God, in you I take refuge;
    save me from all my pursuers and rescue me,
Lest I become like the lion's prey,
    to be torn to pieces, with no one to rescue me.
O Lord, my God, in you I take refuge.
Do me justice, O Lord, because I am just,
    and because of the innocence that is mine.
Let the malice of the wicked come to an end,
    but sustain the just,
    O searcher of heart and soul, O just God.
O Lord, my God, in you I take refuge.
A shield before me is God,
    who saves the upright of heart;
A just judge is God,
    a God who punishes day by day.
O Lord, my God, in you I take refuge.

Fifth Week

OF LENT

Sunday, March 21

This week, we will look at how to move forward so that offenses no longer have power over us or, at least, have less power. At the end of our Lenten study, we want to be changed as a result of the journey we have taken. The change is not just superficial but deep in our hearts. It is out of our hearts that all life flows.

We position ourselves to be heart healthy when we humble ourselves, expect offenses, adjust our expectations, recognize our triggers, and take inventory so that we know what offends us.

....

Pray today that you will be better able to handle offense in your life as a result of your Lenten study. Ask God to know which of the steps you need most to overcome offense.

Monday, March 22

See, days are coming—oracle of the LORD—when I will make a new covenant with the house of Israel and the house of Judah. It will not be like the covenant I made with their ancestors the day I took them by the hand to lead them out of the land of Egypt. They broke my covenant, though I was their master—oracle of the LORD.

—Jeremiah 31:31–32

Through the prophet Jeremiah, God foretells of a future in which he will make a brand new covenant with his people. The covenant will be different from the one made with the Israelites after they were freed from slavery in Egypt. The Israelites were unable to keep the demands of the covenant. They broke the covenant, and once that happened, they came to see God as a master instead of having a personal relationship with him.

God wants us to be free from the sin of offense that enslaves us just as he freed his people from Egypt. And yet, like the Israelites, we can fall back into the slavery of sin by breaking God's commandments.

....

Pray today for the grace to not be enslaved by offense but to live in the freedom God wants for you.

Tuesday, March 23

But this is the covenant I will make with the house of Israel after those days—oracle of the LORD. I will place my law within them, and write it upon their hearts; I will be their God, and they shall be my people.

—Jeremiah 31:33

Through the prophet Jeremiah, God foretells of a new covenant he will form with his people. The law will not just be outside of the people and feel like oppression. God will write the law on their hearts. In his new covenant, his people will want to do his will. They will desire to do his will because they will have a personal relationship with him.

God wants to give us hearts that are free of offense. When God rules and reigns over our hearts then we are no longer easily offended by others' actions. We do not have to look out for our reputations because God, not our own egos, moves to the center of our lives. We no longer have to look out for ourselves because we know God is in charge of our lives.

....

Pray today for a new heart that puts God at the center of your life.

Wednesday, March 24

Or are you unaware that we who were baptized into Christ Jesus were baptized into his death? We were indeed buried with him through baptism into death, so that, just as Christ was raised from the dead by the glory of the Father, we too might live in newness of life.

For if we have grown into union with him through a death like his, we shall also be united with him in the resurrection. We know that our old self was crucified with him, so that our sinful body might be done away with, that we might no longer be in slavery to sin.

—Romans 6:3–6

At our baptism we become united to Jesus. His life becomes our life. Not only does his life become our life but his death becomes our death. We were buried with him so that we could be raised to new life.

We have been united to Christ in his death and are united to him in his Resurrection. Our former selves have been crucified so that we are no longer slaves to sin. Sin is like a parasite that lives in us and feeds off us. But once a body is dead, the parasite no longer feeds off the body. In the same way since we are new creations in Christ, sin no longer feeds off us.

....

We no longer have to be enslaved to the sin of offense because we are new creations in Christ. Take a moment to confess your belief that the old you who held onto offense is dead and that you are a new creation in Christ.

Thursday, March 25
Solemnity of the
Annunciation of the Lord

For a dead person has been absolved from sin. If, then, we have died with Christ, we believe that we shall also live with him. We know that Christ, raised from the dead, dies no more; death no longer has power over him. As to his death, he died to sin once and for all; as to his life, he lives for God. Consequently, you too must think of yourselves as [being] dead to sin and living for God in Christ Jesus.

—Romans 6:7–11

Paul continues to emphasize this truth that we are dead to sin but alive in Christ Jesus. Just as Jesus rose from the dead and lives forever with God, we too are to consider ourselves dead to all sin, including the sin of harboring offenses in our hearts.

The person who is offended when others don't do what they want others to do is dead and alive in Christ Jesus. The person who holds onto past wounds and hurts is dead and alive in Christ Jesus. The person who is offended when others criticize them or give them feedback they don't like is dead and alive in Christ Jesus.

....

Think of yourself as dead to the sin of offense. Say today, "Offense, I am dead to you. You no longer live in me or have power over me. I am alive in Christ Jesus."

Friday, March 26

And do not present the parts of your bodies to sin as weapons for wickedness, but present yourselves to God as raised from the dead to life and the parts of your bodies to God as weapons for righteousness. For sin is not to have any power over you, since you are not under the law but under grace.

—Romans 6:13–14

Paul tells us that we are dead to sin. This is our spiritual reality. However, we still have to choose to live out of this reality. Paul urges us not to yield ourselves to sin but instead yield ourselves to God and how he wants us to act. We are to yield ourselves to God's will and God's way because we have the power of God's grace.

We are no longer under the law but grace. When we see ourselves under the law, we demand our rights. We demand that those who have offended us make it up to us. When we are under the law we are more easily offended. When we live under grace we realize that God has treated us better than we deserve. When we live under grace we recognize that we have the power to yield ourselves to God instead of reacting to what has been done to us.

Thank God today that you don't have to demand or earn your rights. Thank God that he generously gives you his grace.

Saturday, March 27

Jeremiah 31:10, 11–12abcd, 13

The Lord will guard us, as a shepherd guards his flock.

Hear the word of the LORD, O nations,
    proclaim it on distant isles, and say:
He who scattered Israel, now gathers them together,
    he guards them as a shepherd his flock.

The Lord will guard us, as a shepherd guards his flock.

The LORD shall ransom Jacob,
    he shall redeem him from the hand of his
        conqueror.
Shouting, they shall mount the heights of Zion,
    they shall come streaming to the LORD's
        blessings:
The grain, the wine, and the oil,
    the sheep and the oxen.

The Lord will guard us, as a shepherd guards his flock.

Then the virgins shall make merry and dance,
    and young men and old as well.
I will turn their mourning into joy,
    I will console and gladden them after their
        sorrows.

The Lord will guard us, as a shepherd guards his flock.

HOLY WEEK

Sunday, March 28
Palm Sunday of the Passion of the Lord

Today we enter Holy Week and complete our Lenten journey. Our journey leads to the Cross as we remember that Jesus laid down his life so that we might have life. Throughout this week, we will be reflecting on the Cross of Christ and what Jesus accomplished for us.

Each of the gospels offer unique insights into what Jesus' death on the Cross accomplished for us. They look at the same event from different perspectives so that we will have a more complete view of what Jesus suffered and accomplished for us.

....

Ask Jesus to help you grow this week in your appreciation for his work on the Cross.

Monday, March 29

But Jesus cried out again in a loud voice, and gave up his spirit. And behold, the veil of the sanctuary was torn in two from top to bottom.
—Matthew 27:50–51a

In the Temple, there was a place called the Holy of Holies. This was an inner sanctum where the presence of God was said to dwell with the people of Israel. Only the high priest could enter into this place and only once a year on the Day of Atonement. The Holy of Holies was set apart with a huge curtain that was inches thick and dozens of feet tall. It was a symbol of the great divide between God and humans because of the debt we owed God due to sin.

When Jesus died, this curtain was torn in two from top to bottom. God tore the veil of the Temple to show that the divide no longer exists. The debt has been canceled by Jesus' death on the Cross.

....

Thank Jesus for paying your debt so you can freely enter into a relationship with your heavenly Father.

Tuesday, March 30

At noon darkness came over the whole land until three in the afternoon. And at three o'clock Jesus cried out in loud voice, "*Eloi, Eloi, lema sabachthani?*" which is translated, "My God, my God, why have you forsaken me?"

—Mark 15:33–34

Sin brings about a three-fold alienation or separation. Sin separates us from ourselves as we no longer feel comfortable in our own skin. Sin alienates us from other people as we are at war with others. And sin alienates us from God. Jesus on the Cross felt the full weight of this alienation. He was abandoned by his closest friends and then felt the separation from his heavenly Father.

....

Jesus, who never sinned, experienced the pain of sin so that we could have a relationship with our heavenly Father. Thank Jesus today for experiencing that alienation so that you could live in relationship with God and others.

Wednesday, March 31

Now one of the criminals hanging there reviled Jesus, saying, "Are you not the Messiah? Save yourself and us." The other, however, rebuking him, said in reply, "Have you no fear of God, for you are subject to the same condemnation? And indeed, we have been condemned justly, for the sentence we received corresponds to our crimes, but this man has done nothing criminal." Then he said, "Jesus, remember me when you come into your kingdom." He replied to him, "Amen, I say to you, today you will be with me in Paradise."
—Luke 23:39–43

People who were crucified ultimately died from suffocation. As they hung on the cross, fluid would pour into their lungs. A man hanging on a cross had to continually pull himself up just to catch a breath. For every breath Jesus took on the Cross, he had to expend a great deal of energy. It cost Jesus dearly to answer the other criminal on the cross.

The thief on the cross was a criminal. He deserved to die, as he noted; but by simply asking Jesus to remember him in his kingdom, he receives eternal life.

We cannot earn eternal life. We cannot earn the Paradise of heaven. We can't earn it, but we can receive it because of Jesus' work on the Cross.

....

Take a moment to pray with the good thief. Pray today, "Jesus, remember me when you come into your kingdom."

Thursday, April 1
Holy Thursday

There they crucified him, and with him two others,
one on either side, with Jesus in the middle. Pilate
also had an inscription written and put on the cross.
It read, "Jesus the Nazorean, the King of the Jews."
—John 19:18–19

When the Romans crucified a man, they would put the charge over his head. Pilate wrote that Jesus is the King of the Jews. Jesus had resisted this title throughout his ministry and even through his trial, but here on the Cross Jesus is proclaimed king.

Jesus is proclaimed king on the Cross when he performs his ultimate act of service for us. He does not use his kingship to control and manipulate others but to serve us and bring us into a relationship with his Father.

....

Take a moment to acknowledge Christ as your king. Thank him for his work and service on the Cross.

Friday, April 2
Good Friday of the Passion of the Lord

After this, aware that everything was now finished, in order that scripture might be fulfilled, Jesus said, "I thirst." There was a vessel filled with common wine. So they put a sponge soaked in wine on a sprig of hyssop and put it up to his mouth. When Jesus had taken the wine, he said, "It is finished." And bowing his head, he handed over the spirit.

—John 19:28–30

John tells us of Jesus' last words. Jesus says he thirsts. He thirsts for a relationship with us. He thirsts for our wholeness and well-being that we will move beyond the offenses we have suffered into the better life he has prepared for us.

Then Jesus says, "It is finished." He doesn't mean that he is finished, but that his redemptive work has been completed. He fully surrendered his life in order to pay our debt.

....

How do we respond to the incredible gift of Jesus' death? We can begin with a simple thank you. It seems so small and so simple, but it is a way we can respond to his gift. Thank Jesus today for surrendering his life in order that you may have life.

Saturday, April 3
Holy Saturday

Psalm 22:8–9, 17–18, 19–20, 23–24

My God, my God, why have you abandoned me?

All who see me scoff at me;
    they mock me with parted lips, . . .
"He relied on the LORD; let him deliver him,
    let him rescue him, if he loves him."

My God, my God, why have you abandoned me?

Indeed, many dogs surround me,
    a pack of evildoers closes in upon me;
they have pierced my hands and my feet;
    I can count all my bones.

My God, my God, why have you abandoned me?

They divide my garments among them,
    and for my vesture they cast lots.
But you, O LORD, be not far from me;
    O my help, hasten to aid me.

My God, my God, why have you abandoned me?

I will proclaim you name to my brethren;
    in the midst of the assembly I will praise you:
"You who fear the LORD, praise him;
    all you descendants of Jacob, give glory to him;
    revere him, all you descendants of Israel!"

My God, my God, why have you abandoned me?

Rev. Michael White and **Tom Corcoran** are coauthors of the bestselling Rebuilt Parish series, including the award-winning *Rebuilt, Tools for Rebuilding, Rebuilding Your Message, The Rebuilt Field Guide,* and *ChurchMoney.* White serves as pastor and Corcoran as pastoral associate at Church of the Nativity in the Archdiocese of Baltimore. Together, they lead the Rebuilt Parish Association. They are the hosts of the CatholicTV series, *The Rebuilt Show.* White and Corcoran have spoken at conferences and parishes throughout the United States and Canada and at diocesan gatherings and conferences in Austria, Australia, Germany, Ireland, Poland, and Switzerland. They have been guests on EWTN, CatholicTV, Salt + Light Television, and numerous Catholic radio programs.

churchnativity.com
rebuiltparish.com
rebuiltparish.podbean.com/
Facebook: churchnativity
Twitter: @churchnativity
Instagram: @churchnativity

AVE

AVE MARIA PRESS

Founded in 1865, Ave Maria Press,
a ministry of the Congregation of
Holy Cross, is a Catholic publishing
company that serves the spiritual and
formative needs of the Church and its
schools, institutions, and ministers;
Christian individuals and families; and
others seeking spiritual nourishment.

———

For a complete listing of titles from

Ave Maria Press

Sorin Books

Forest of Peace

Christian Classics

visit avemariapress.com